I0504890

Management Without Reservations:
Leadership Principles for the Manager's Life Journey

Management Without Reservations: Leadership Principles for the Manager's Life Journey

✦

25 Life-Shaping Principles for Successful Leaders

Brother Herman Zaccarelli, C.S.C.

iUniverse, Inc.

New York Lincoln Shanghai

Management Without Reservations: Leadership Principles for the Manager's Life Journey
25 Life-Shaping Principles for Successful Leaders

Copyright © 2007 by Brother Herman Zaccarelli

All rights reserved. No part of this book may be used or reproduced by any means, graphic, electronic, or mechanical, including photocopying, recording, taping or by any information storage retrieval system without the written permission of the publisher except in the case of brief quotations embodied in critical articles and reviews.

iUniverse books may be ordered through booksellers or by contacting:

iUniverse
2021 Pine Lake Road, Suite 100
Lincoln, NE 68512
www.iuniverse.com
1-800-Authors (1-800-288-4677)

The views expressed in this work are solely those of the author and do not necessarily reflect the views of the publisher, and the publisher hereby disclaims any responsibility for them.

Cameron W. Watson, President of Fluid Media, Atlanta GA., and his creative team are responsible for the book's cover graphics and design.

ISBN: 978-0-595-44053-5 (pbk)
ISBN: 978-0-595-88376-9 (ebk)

Printed in the United States of America

Don't ask yourself what the world needs; ask yourself what makes you come alive, and go do that, because what the world needs are people who have come alive.

—Gil Bailie

This book is dedicated to Bill Myers, a man who is joyfully alive and from whom this world has immensely benefited.

Founder, owner, and president of Franchise Management Systems, Bill, and his lovely wife Adele, are my long-time friends. Bill epitomizes the joy that can be found in being fully alive through life's journey. It is his spirit of joyful living I sought to capture in this book.

I met Bill over 40 years ago. We shared the same interest in the hospitality industry. But, as the decades passed, Bill would ultimately be found to be far different from others that I met. In addition to sharp business skills, he possessed, and readily displayed a sensitivity and compassion toward his employees and customers that I came to find was rare indeed. Some would maintain that, having chosen business as a vocation, such a man would inevitably change over time. Bill never changed.

A person of unusual depth and strength of character, Bill's energy, generosity and devotion to his industry, his family, and his community have never failed to stir in me a sense of profound respect and admiration.

When I undertook this writing project, I looked for an example of a book that I felt would capture the perception, the wisdom and the compassion that can be gained over a life's journey enthusiastically and honorably lived. I felt such a book could serve as a model for my own efforts. I did not find such a book. I didn't need to. I had already found Bill. His life, lived fully, is the model for this book.

John of Salisbury, the 12th. century Bishop of Chartes spoke of Bill long ago when he stated,

> *We are like dwarfs perched upon the shoulders of giants. We see more than our predecessors, not because we have a keener vision or greater height, we are lifted up and borne on their gigantic stature.*

With the warmest of personal regards, this book is dedicated to Bill Myers, a giant of a man, who is as alive as I hope readers will find this manuscript's humble effort to capture his essence.

Contents

Section 4 It's About Serving Your Customers

Section 5 It's About Knowing Your Goals

Acknowledgements

No one writes a book alone. The phrase "It Takes A Village" is certainly true in the development of books and this one is no exception. I am deeply grateful to those many friends and colleagues who helped bring this special manuscript to full fruition.

David K. Hayes, Ph.D., an accomplished author, as well as his wife (and my dear friend!) Peggy, were instrumental in the completion of this project's final phase. They added tremendously to my efforts.

I also am indebted to Dr. Jack Ninemeier, a life-long colleague, whose wisdom has proven invaluable in many instances, including this important occasion. I am especially grateful to Russ Pottle, President, Tennessee Bookman Company, Fairview, TN, who has assisted me with his publishing expertise over many years, Special thanks go to Peter D. Moore, Vice President; Capegemini, Cambridge, MA., as well as Robert Truck, President; Outsourcing Group, Fairless Hills, PA, and Donald Christie, M.B.A., President of American Financial and Tax Shoppe, Winter Park, Fl. and Jim Evans, President, Opus Group, Scottsdale, AZ. Without these individuals, the project would not have attained the level of quality it now possesses.

In addition to those who assisted in the book's production, I want to thank the individual who inspired me to bring it into being. Brother Dennis Fleming C.S.C., Administrator of Christopher Lodge, Cocoa Beach, Fl., whose collaborative management style stimulated me to complete this book, is that individual. It is my hope that the ideas and insights I have presented in this volume justly honor him.

Finally, to the administrators and my colleagues at Barry University, who have supported me in all of my educational endeavors, I offer my heartfelt gratitude. They have enriched my life and, it is my wish that through this book, permitted me to humbly seek to enrich the lives of others. If readers feel I have done so, this book will be the success all of the individuals named on this page so richly deserve.

Foreword

Few things are more pleasing than touring an unfamiliar location with a knowledgeable local guide. You know the type; they are at once educated, entertaining, sometimes irreverent, but always fascinating and never to be forgotten. From the opening pages of *Management Without Reservations: Leadership Principles for the Manager's Life Journey*, you quickly realize that Brother Herman Zaccarelli C.S.C. is just such a guide. As a distinctive manager and leader with 50 plus years of experience, his book contains nothing less than the extraordinary observations of a decidedly optimistic and insightful observer of the unique human condition.

In *Management Without Reservations*, Zaccarelli takes his readers to the out of the way places of management thought, known only to those who are intimately familiar with the territory. With the deep understanding of life for which he is well known, he leads readers on a absorbing Five-stop, and always fascinating, journey through the province of management and leadership.

Beginning with the perceptive observation that before studying management, managers must first study themselves, (*It's About Who You Are*), the author next illustrates the importance of managerial action (*It's About What You Do*). Recognizing that leaders accomplish little without the backing of those they lead, (*It's About Building Your Team*) is the next stop. Zaccarelli then lingers, and ponders insightfully, the critical importance of serving others (*It's About Serving Customers*). The excursion concludes with a final, and satisfying, stop at better understanding your own life aspirations (*It's About Knowing Your Goals*). All along the way, Zaccarelli shares his unabashed management vision via 25 key managerial and leadership principles.

Written in a direct and immensely readable style, readers will quickly feel "at home" with the text's contemplative "Think It Through" and "Personal Challenge" sections, which add greatly to the book's easy to read, easy to understand and easy to remember style.

Don't expect an ordinary tour guide on this fascinating excursion. Zaccarelli eagerly and enthusiastically shows you the world he loves and, like the best of guides, he clearly loves doing it. Your guide is lively, quick and just as apt to point out sights along the way that draw from the views of management theorist Peter Drucker as he is the psychological insights of Harvard professor B.F. Skinner or, true to his eclectic nature, the biting wit of Mae West.

In this indispensable guide for experienced as well as novice travelers in the management world, Zaccarelli deftly and knowledgably points out the traits of wisdom, courage, and love of the dynamic that mark the realm he has traveled and knows so well. He is the type of exceptional guide who must be followed if you wish to someday, in a grand manner, travel without reservations in your own managerial world. Get ready for an adventure, because this book is nothing less than an all expense paid ticket for a trip you will never forget.

Jack D. Ninemeier Ph.D.
Professor
Eli Broad Graduate School of Management
Michigan State University

Section 1

It's About Who You Are

1

Be a Visionary: Know where you are going

It's Essential:

Consider the challenge you would face if, right now, you wished to travel to a specific address in New York City. Like many Americans, you probably recognize that one of the easiest ways to find out how to get there would be to Google "Mapquest" or some other website designed to provide you directions; enter your current location (where you are right now), and then type in the address of where you want to go.

You can do it easily … if you know exactly where you are and where you want to be.

If, however, you don't really know where you wish to go, it is impossible to use the Internet tools available to you to get there.

Mapquest gives you all the specific information you need to arrive in your desired location. It includes the names of the highways and roads you will take, the right and left hand turns you must make, and even the distance and time required between each step in your journey, thus avoiding mistakes and wasted time.

Life's journey, as well as your management career, is very much like traveling. To be the most successful manager you can possibly be, it is essential that you understand where you are now. You also must be able to clearly identify where you want to be, if you ever hope to get there.

1. Have you ever wanted to take a trip to somewhere new? _____?

2. Would you begin such a trip not knowing where you wanted to end up? _____?

3. If you did not know your final destination, how would you make plans to get there? _____

Successful Managers Know ...

Life is often lived backwards. In most cases, you must be able to see your end goal before you can begin planning how to achieve it. As soon as you determine your destination, however, the scheduling, tools, timing and actions you must take to get there become much clearer to you.

When you identify precisely what you intend to accomplish as a manager, the steps you must take to reach your goals will become as clear to you as Mapquest directions are to its users. You will know the roads to take, the turns to make, and how long it will likely take to get there.

Whether your management vision involves achieving financial objectives, enhancing your community, improving personal relationships at work, the achievement of specific service levels, or any other measurable objective, your vision should have definitive traits. It must be:

• Identifiable

• Communicable

- Inspiring

- Rewarding

When your vision has these characteristics, you will know where you are going and be able to lead others there as well.

Think It Through

1. As a manager, do you have definite ideas about the goals you seek to achieve? _____.

2. List your current top three goals:

   a. _____

   b. _____

   c. _____

3. Could you easily explain to others the reasons your goals are important? _____

4. Do you think you could secure the wholehearted assistance of others in meeting your goals if you could not explain them? _____

Personal Challenges

- I will always make sure I am firmly aware of precisely what I seek to achieve as a manager.

- I will evaluate all of my work-related actions and decisions based on their ability to help me reach my managerial goals.

2

Be a Leader:
Know how to take others with you

It's Essential:

In the simplest terms, leaders can be described as persons who know where they want to go, who get up, and who go! Of course, great leaders do even more. They inspire followers who go with them.

The simple fact is that, in most significant human endeavors, a group of people can accomplish far more than can any one individual.

Consider, for example, the process required to build an airplane. The actual construction of a plane is a remarkable thing. The talent required to build an airplane includes individuals skilled in aerodynamics, metallurgy, welding, electronics, computer programming and interior design, to name but a few areas.

The most important thing to know about building an airplane, however, is that a leader, who understands the building team's end-goal, must direct the process.

Interestingly, the individual leading the team building the airplane may not be an expert at any one area of airplane construction. They must, however, be an expert leader.

Even if the leader did have all of the skills necessary to build the plane themselves, the time it would take to do so proves the importance of group effort when undertaking complex activities; the precise kind of activities you manage everyday at work.

---

1. Consider the work of an orchestra conductor. Do they play music or lead music? _____

2. Do you think the conductor in an orchestra could play each of the instruments as well as the person whose job it is to play it? _____?

3. Do you think it would be possible for the conductor, even if tremendously talented, to play, at the same time, all of the musical instruments needed to beautifully perform one of Beethoven's symphonies? _____

Successful Managers Know ...

That there are three crucial components of effective leadership:

First, leaders must carefully and clearly explain their own vision of the group's intended destination to each individual member of the team.

Secondly, leaders must make sure each group member understands just how critical a role he or she plays in the goals the team seeks to achieve.

Thirdly, group members must be absolutely clear about how they will personally benefit as the group strives to reach its goals. Too often, managers emphasize how the company or organization will benefit from the hard work of its members. It may well be so, but the individual must know they benefit as well.

Great leaders understand that passionate followers become passionate only when they are fully and personally committed. As a result, leadership can be viewed as no more or less than creating trust in followers.

Great leaders create exceptional levels of trust and excitement. These leaders are followed because their followers want to reap all of the benefits that accrue to those who are allowed membership in the group.

Think It Through

1. Consider the team you belong to. Has your own leader identified how following his or her lead benefits you personally?_____

2. As a leader how important is it for you to be able to identify the benefits that will accrue to your group members? _____.

3. Do you believe each team member you lead can be motivated? _____

4. Assume that money is only one of the rewards that membership in your group brings to its members. Identify three alternative benefits that your own group members gain by following where you lead them.

   a. _____

   b. _____

   c. _____

Personal Challenges

- I will remember to continually explain to my team where we are going and why it is so important that we get there.

- In the case of every team member for which I am responsible, I will make it a point to remind that individual how they benefit personally when our team reaches its goals.

3

Be a Student: Keep learning

It's Essential:

Perceptive people know that there is a natural tendency toward the decay, or breaking down, of nearly all aspects of our world. As a result, much of the time spent by a society's members involves counteracting this interesting phenomenon called entropy. Entropy simply means that any system or organization that is not continually maintained will deteriorate.

Consider the lawn at your home. If the grass is watered, trimmed, and fertilized, it will grow and stay a beautiful lawn.

If, however, you stop caring for it, weeds will appear, the grass will likely die out, and the lawn itself will deteriorate. Place an automobile in the same yard and leave it alone for ten years, and you will see the same forces of entropy slowly convert the car to a rusting hunk of unusable metal.

The result of society's active battle to counter entropy is that the world continually changes. As it changes, you too must change to keep up, because with change
comes new knowledge, new ways of doing things, and new ways of seeing your
world. That is why it is especially essential that you be keenly aware of the evolu-
tionary nature of your own surroundings.

---

1. Consider the automobile you own now compared to the first one you
    ever owned. Are the systems in your current vehicle more compli-
    cate than those of your first car? _____

2. How much time and money per month do you, or your mechanic,
    spend doing routine maintenance on you car? (for example, oil
    changes, fluid checks, washing, and the like).
    Time: _____?
    Money: _____?

3. What would likely happen if, for the next 12 months, you decided to
    spend nothing at all to maintain your vehicle, yet drove it as often as
    you do now? _____

Successful Managers Know …

That sometimes employees view their supervisors as the ones who "Know it all."

In many cases, a supervisor or manager may in fact have earned their position
because they know a lot and are very skilled at what they do.

The most knowledgeable managers, however, when asked, will readily tell you
that the more they know, the more they recognize their need to know more.

Moreover, they take the steps needed to continue their learning.

As a manager, the number of ways you can "keep current" are many. They
include reading professional journals and trade magazines, subscriptions to on-
line newsletters that target your industry, and reading on a wide variety of work-
related topics.

As well, attendance at professional trade shows and conferences, participation in
employer-sponsored training opportunities, networking with colleagues, and

seeking the advice of bosses who can direct you to additional sources of information are all-important learning options.

There is no limit to the learning choices you will have. However, how you seek to learn is much less important than your desire to seek learning. Remember that, in today's rapidly changing work environments, the managers who do not "know it all" are <u>not</u> the ones who will fail. Rather, failure will befall those managers who do not seek to learn continually, because the forces of change will surely leave them behind.

Think It Through

1. Has the business that you are in changed much from when you first started in it? _____.

2. Who do you believe is responsible for ensuring that you are fully informed about recent and future changes occurring in your field? _____

3. Consider the last three months; what specific self-initiated professional development tasks did you complete? _____

4. Re-consider your own professional development. What are three specific ways you can keep your own knowledge level up-to-date?

   a. _____

   b. _____

   c. _____

Personal Challenges

- I will make it one of my priorities to recall that, to be fair to myself, I need to regularly take time out to learn.

- I will make sure that, at least once per quarter, I point out specific learning opportunities for every member of my organization who reports directly to me.

4

Be a Teacher:
Share your knowledge

It's Essential:

If you live in a house or an apartment, you probably have a food freezer. You have it so you can fill it with food. That's because you know that the essential function of a food freezer is to hold food until you want it and really need it.

When the freezer temperature is kept at "zero" degrees Fahrenheit (-17 degrees Celsius) or lower, your freezer will perform its function well.

But, it is most important to understand that the whole point of having a freezer is not to fill it, but rather to empty it.

Gathering knowledge is much like filling a freezer. It is important to gather and retain as much as you can. However, the real value of knowledge becomes most clear when you can take it out and apply it at a time you really need it.

In life, there are many individuals with great knowledge. Their freezers are full. But consider the wasted potential if their knowledge was never shared. It would be similar to a remarkable musical composer who never wrote music, a Gold-medal quality athlete who did not compete, or the Grand Master painter who never pick up a brush. In fact, the ability to share and thus pass on learning among ourselves is one of the key characteristics that distinguishes humans from all other species on the planet.

1. Think of an activity that you can do really well. _____

2. What are some words that would describe how you would likely feel if someone asked you to teach them, or give them tips, about how you do it?_____, _____, _____.

3. What are some words that would describe how that person would likely feel if, when asked, you refused to share your knowledge with them? _____, _____,

     _____.

Successful Managers Know ...

That one very useful definition of "**Manage**" is:

"The ability to direct others with a high degree of skill".

As a result, depending upon the specific team of individuals for which you are responsible, when you manage them well, you have the opportunity to multiply your influence times the number of people you direct.

From a practical perspective, however, there are really only two ways to direct another's behavior.

You can either tell them what to do or teach them what to do.

Interestingly, some managers feel they simply do not have the time to teach, so they prefer to "tell." And they have to do it over and over!

That's because the process of "telling" people what to do will get the work done, but it never builds to something better. When employees have not been taught, they most often will wait to be told. It's pretty clear that if you make the effort to teach others, you not only save time, you increase your team's efficiency. That is so because you will not always be around when your employees need to know what to do. As a result, teaching them to act on their own lets them keep working,…. rather than wait for you.

Those who do not teach also seem to have missed the point that knowledge is one of the few things in life that you can give to others and still have just as much as when you started.

Think It Through

1. How often does it happen that your staff members make a wrong decision? _____.

2. Do you think they would have made the same decision if they had talked to you about it first? _____.

3. Think about your answer to the two questions above. Why do you think the employee failed to consult you?
   _____

4. Consider your own time commitments. What are three things you could, in the short run, delegate to others so you could spend more of your valuable time teaching.

   a. _____

   b. _____

   c. _____

Personal Challenges

- I will rely on teaching, more than telling, to make my own work team more effective.

- I will make sure every person reporting to me understands that teaching those whom they directly manage is one of their critical responsibilities.

5

Embrace Change:
Be adaptable

It's Essential:

It's been said that babies are the only ones who truly embrace change!

The reality of life, for most people, is that change continually occurs; and that sometimes it is appreciated and sometimes not. The difference in appreciated change and change that is not appreciated can often be traced back to the source of the change.

When change is forced upon us, we often find it uncomfortable, daunting, intimidating, or even scary. As a result, we sometimes tend to resist it.

However, when the change is self-initiated, it is most often better accepted. In fact, rather than resist change, true *"Change-makers"* actively seek out areas of their lives, and their world, where they can make positive changes.

Change is essential because the healthy person, the one who lives life to its fullest, craves an occasional zaniness, a departure from the ordinary, his or her own festival of excitement, and sometimes, a new way of living life. Change brings exactly that.

Consider the last time you ordered food in a restaurant:

1. Would it have been your preference to order for yourself, or to let someone you just met order for you? _____

2. How do you think you would have felt if someone ordered for you and you did not like the choice? _____?

3. Do you believe you generally have a very high degree of interest in making change-related decisions that affect you, or a low degree of interest in doing so? _____

Successful Managers Know ...

There is a tongue-in-cheek definition of "insanity". You have probably heard that;

> *"Insanity consists of doing the same thing over and over and expecting a different result".*

As an effective manager, if you want to achieve results that are different from those you now achieve, you must change what you and your team are doing.

Good managers aggressively seek out those areas that need improvement. These might include guest service levels, revenue targets, interpersonal relationships, productivity measures or a variety of other ways effectiveness is judged.

When they have determined where improvements should be made, these managers next examine their current way of doing things, and then they implement the changes that need to be put in place to achieve better results.

Experimentation, innovation, and an open mind are all tools effective managers use to embrace change and thus achieve improved performance. Those who try new things may not always achieve better results on their first try, but much of the time, they will. Even when it requires several tries, they will always be better off than managers who are simply content to suffer with the current level of "insanity".

Think It Through

1. Are there any areas for which you are responsible where the results produced are consistently below your expectation levels?
   _____.

2. Are there effective tools to measure performance change in those areas? _____.

3. Is it part of your job to help initiate positive change?
   _____

4. What are three specific areas within your organization that could benefit from proactive change you can initiate?

   a. _____

   b. _____

   c. _____

Personal Challenges

- I will consistently explain to others that proactive change will result in improvement, if not the first time we try, then the next time.

- I will remember to secure the involvement and, as a result, the commitment of others before initiating significant change.

Section 2

It's About What You Do

6

Be Organized:
In Your Own Way

It's Essential:

Have you ever misplaced your car keys? If you are like most people, your answer is ... Yes!

How much time, effort (and aggravation!) have you expended looking for lost car keys ... (or TV remotes,.... eyeglasses, or telephone numbers?). Again, if you are like most people, your answer is "Way too much!"

Invariably, you spend time looking for car keys when you are already running behind.

The result? You run even further behind.

The real question, of course, is why do most people, time after time, spend so much effort thinking "behind" instead of thinking "ahead"?

When you think ahead, you are taking the time to make yourself aware of how what you do now will affect what you do in the future.

When you think behind, you are desperately trying to recall what you did and why you did it. It is not a pleasant activity.

Organized people think ahead. They may spend a bit more of their time doing so, but they spend a lot less of their time thinking "behind."

---

1. One of the best things about getting older is the realization that it's O.K. to be yourself. For example, think about the clothes you like to wear best. How do you feel when you are dressed in those clothes? _____

2. Do you wear them most often because they impress others, or because they make you feel comfortable? _____

3. Would you wear those clothes less often if a friend told you that they, personally, liked other clothes better? _____

Successful Managers Know ...

Assume that someone asked you to define the word "organized".

What words would immediately come to mind? Would they be?

- Straightened?

- Tidy?

- In a row?

- Color Coded?

- Sorted?

- Perfectly filed?

- Messy?

All of the above words *could* be associated with organization, or with organized people, but they do not describe the only ways to be organized. You may consider yourself well organized, or you may not.

True organization really consists of only two things:

1. Having a system that works for you

2. Understanding how your own system can be used to help you achieve your management goals

Whether or not others easily recognize your system of organization is not very important. The organizational style that naturally fits you is the one that will most often work best for you. If tidy works, be tidy. If lists work, use lists. If 100 stacks of paper works for you, start stacking.

Managers rarely have enough time in the day to achieve all they wish to achieve. Regardless of your approach to organizing what you do, save time by using your time to think ahead, not behind.

Think It Through

1. Despite differences in outward appearances, do you believe all managers must engage in planning ahead if they are to be most effective? _____.

2. Do you consider your organizational skills to be among your strongest skills? _____.

3. What would the likely consequences be if your organizational skills were improved? _____

4. Consider your own organizational skills. List three specific steps you could take to better help yourself "get organized".

    a. _____

    b. _____

    c. _____

Personal Challenges

- A focus on thinking ahead can help prevent thinking behind. I will remember that proper planning and forward thinking improves my own managerial performance.

- Some people I work with seem more organized than others. I will make sure I focus on the results achieved by my team members' organizational skills, and not solely on the outward appearance of those skills.

7

Keep Your Focus:
Customers vs. competitors

It's Essential:

Some of the most common analogies used in business relate to sports and war. Thus, managers are exhorted to "Win", to "Be First", to "Keep Your Eye on the Ball" or to utilize strategies and tactics designed to excel at the "Art" of war.

It's unfortunate that such analogies exist, because perceptive managers understand that businesses that spend too much time focusing on competitors most often lose focus on their own customers.

Coca Cola and Pepsi know that there is room in the market for both. Each will succeed best not when they "beat" or "destroy" the other. They will thrive best when they understand that providing value to their customers is about listening, the interchange of ideas, responsiveness and cooperation. Each of these requires that managers focus their efforts internally and cooperatively on their customers, not externally or competitively on what their rivals are doing.

If there is any value to a sports and business analogy, it may come from the coach who, when asked what he thought about the team that he was going to play next replied, "I never think about our opponents and what they can do. I focus on our team and what we should do!" That coach is a true winner!

---

1. Consider the company that provides service to your cell phone. Are you completely satisfied with them? _____

2. Do you think they would provide better service to you if they had fewer competitors _____?

3. If you were the leader of the company that provides your cell phone service, would you instruct members of your organization to spend more of their time monitoring competitors or listening to the needs of your current customers?_____

Successful Managers Know ...

You have probably heard the saying "America loves a winner." Perhaps that's true in sports, but fortunately for most of us, it simply is not true in business. Consumers don't love a winner, they love themselves. And because they do, they reward those companies and businesses that seek, above all else, to give their customers what they really want.

If you are old enough, you probably remember the Avis commercial that included the line "We're Number 2, so we try harder!" In response to this advertisement, America loved not the #1 car rental company, but the "little" guy who tried harder by putting the wants of their customer's first.

Think about your own customers. Would they rather do business with a company that:

Is most efficient?

Generates the highest profit?

Provides the greatest Return on Investment (ROI) to its owners?

Recognizes their customer's needs and concentrates on meeting them?

Your customer's definitions of value can vary greatly. For some, value means highest quality, for others, lowest price, while still others may value time-savings, durability or a host of other characteristics. In all cases, however, those managers who concentrate on providing value to their customers stay in business, those who do not ... do not.

Think It Through

1. Businesses do not exist to make a profit. They exist to serve customers. Consider a business you knew of, but that no longer exists. Did they have a "customer first" attitude?

   _____.

2. Who supplies profits to a business? That is, in whose pocket was the money businesses report as profits, before it was placed in the business's bank account? _____.

3. If you receive exceptional value from a product or service you purchase, are you concerned about the profit level achieved by the company from whom you made the purchase?

   _____

4. Does it make sense to you that the companies that achieve the highest profit levels will be those who provide the greatest customer value? _____

Personal Challenges

- Many companies that once led their fields no longer exist because, while they thought they knew exactly what their customers wanted, in fact they did not. I will simply not let that happen to me and my team.

- Change can be difficult, but when it is called for, I will make sure I support all of the efforts required to make the changes valued by my customers.

8

Maintain Your Standards:
Be a positive example

It's Essential:

<u>The Boy Who Cried Wolf</u>, is a well-known fable by Aesop, the Greek slave and storyteller who lived from 620-560 BC. In the fable, a bored shepherd boy entertains himself by calling out "wolf" even though his flock is not under attack. Nearby villagers who came to his rescue found that the alarms were false and that they'd wasted their time. Later, when the boy was actually confronted by a wolf, the villagers did not believe his cries for help and his flock perished. The moral of the fable, is often stated as:

Even when liars tell the truth, they are never believed.

Interestingly enough, people who read the story often miss the second, but related, lesson Aesops's story delivers. It is simply this:

People will believe you are truthful, only until they discover you lie.

For those in leadership positions, it isn't possible to demonstrate high standards of integrity *most* of the time. They must be displayed *all* of the time. An individual's credibility only rises to the lowest occasion on which others observed it, not the highest. Because that is true, it is important to understand that the positive examples leaders seek to demonstrate must be displayed consistently and on *every* occasion in which they are observed.

1. Assume for a moment that you need a very important favor done for you. The favor is not hard to do, nor will it take long. However, it is absolutely critical that it be done at a very specific time and on a very specific date. Whom among your current friends would you most trust to remember to do the favor and to ensure absolutely that it would be done on time? _____

2. What is it in your history with that person that convinces you they would be the best choice of a reliable person that you can confidently count on? _____

3. Would your view of that person be different if, on more than one occasion in the past, they had promised to do something for you but did not keep their promise? _____.

Successful Managers Know ...

Consider the ethical standards you hope your team displays when dealing with customers or otherwise completing their work.

Are these characteristics that you yourself are capable of consistently demonstrating? Too often managers feel that by setting their standards exceptionally high, followers will be better motivated to achieve those standards.

High standards are desirable. However, if the standards are set so high that you, as the leader, often fall short, especially in ways that are easily observed by your followers, the results can be disastrous.

Setting high standards does nothing. *Attaining* high standards is what makes the impact on others. Standards must be attained 100% of the time or they serve to de-motivate employees, because when leaders fall short, followers consider the failure acceptable.

It has been said that the faults of the people stem from the faults of their leaders. In reality, the faults of the leaders are reflected in their people. Management without reservations means having realistic, not artificially high, expectations for your own standards and for yourself.

For leaders, the bottom line is this: setting high standards for others and then failing, personally, to maintain them is like being the boy who cried wolf. You simply won't be believed, … about your standards, … or anything else.

Think It Through

1. Managers know that employees observe the actions of their leaders intensely. Do you believe those you lead look to you for examples of "acceptable and unacceptable" behavior?
   _____.

2. How do you think your employees would react if they saw you do something that you had previously indicated to them was improper or even offensive? _____.

3. How do you think they would they react if, in defense of your improper behavior, you said to them "Do as I say, … not as I do?
   _____

4. List three specific areas in which you truly want your employees to use your own actions as their role model.

   a. _____

   b. _____

   c. _____

Personal Challenges

- Personal credibility is one of a manager's most valuable assets. I will maintain my credibility with others by consistently displaying the standards I publicly endorse.

- No one is perfect. Not even me. If I do fail to maintain the standards I have set for myself and others, I will accept the responsibility for my own actions and vow to do better in the future.

9

Consider All Viewpoints:
Be open minded

It's Essential:

Risk and uncertainty make people very uncomfortable. Risk avoidance has created a $1.5 trillion dollar insurance industry worldwide. It is why car rental companies will often make more money on the "collision damage insurance" they sell than they do renting cars. It is why buyers of appliances such as microwaves, stereos, cell phones and the like will spend large sums of money on extended warranties of questionable value. It is why criminals and prosecutors plea-bargain, each being unsure about what a jury would actually do.

Risk aversion also plays an important part in personal decision-making. Because people seek, naturally, to avoid risk, they also frequently tend to choose what is familiar, do what is expected, and in general make decisions inside their own comfort zone.

It is a truism, however, that great advancements occur when people move decisively outside the tried and true and venture into the unknown. In fact, most great discoveries were, at one time, considered absolutely impossible. Airplane flight, human organ transplants, space travel, and wireless Internet access are just a few examples. In a similar manner, if you are to make great advances in your own life, you must stay open-minded to consider all of the possibilities; even those that are impossible. Improvements are the result of an open-mind.

---

1. Assume that you were asked to contribute $1.00 to buy a lottery ticket with a 50/50 chance of winning $1,000,000.00. Would you do it? _____

2. Most people are willing to risk a little for the chance to win a lot. Do you think that is why casinos are so popular?
    _____

3. If they are honest, most people will tell you they understand that, over the long run, casinos make their profits by paying out less in winnings than is paid in to them in bets. Given that, why do you think casino gambling remains such a rapidly growing industry?
    _____

Successful Managers Know ...

In business, embracing viewpoints that lead to innovation, change and creativity does not mean that managers ignore risk. Rather, it is the intelligent acceptance of risk that separates open-minded managers from those who are not.

The relationship between risk and reward is well known by those in business. In all business investment, for example, increased risk level offers increased reward levels.

Managing without reservation means recognizing and controlling risk, not completely avoiding it. An intelligence assessment of managerial risk can be likened to jumping from a bridge with a bungee cord. The exhilarating reward derived from bungee cord jumping accrues only to those brave enough and intelligent enough to thoroughly check out their equipment before they welcome the excitement of the jump.

Increased reward in nearly all aspects of business is often accompanied by the assumption of greater challenge, increased cost and the unknown. With that in mind, it is important to realize that these risks can be anticipated, and they can be managed. In fact, when you are not afraid, you can calmly assess all viewpoints presented to you with an open mind, and be the creative, innovative manager that makes spectacular, even impossible progress possible.

Think It Through

1. Successful managers understand that one of their greatest dangers is taking too many precautions. Doing so is one trait of closed-minded people. Since most people tend to act in ways they sincerely believe to be their own best interest, why do you think some close-minded managers stay that way? _____.

2. In your own area of expertise, what do you think would be the end-result of managers who continually refuse to embrace new ideas and the change they inevitably bring? _____.

3. Do you believe you are considered by your peers as quite open to listening to new ideas that could significantly advance your organization's goals? _____

4. Consider those people whom you believe to be very open-minded. Name three specific traits they consistently display that convinces you they are willing to truly consider new ideas without being overly critical of those ideas they do not ultimately accept:

   a. _____

   b. _____

   c. _____

Personal Challenges

• Little can be accomplished if all possible objections must be overcome before starting. I will do my best to look for the reasons why, instead of why not, when presented with a new idea.

- Whenever I start feeling too cautious, I will recall that even a turtle, slow and deliberate as it may be, only makes progress when it sticks its neck out.

10

Make Your Own Decisions: Great managers are decisive

It's Essential:

It is interesting to observe that, in nearly all cases, those leaders who command great followings are those who lead decisively. In fact, determined leadership and the decision-making it requires are almost universally present in great leaders. Decisiveness is also one of a leader's most visible traits. People immediately recognize decisiveness.

Of course, it's simple to make choices decisively when they are easy and everyone agrees with them. What is rarer, but much more valuable, is the leader who will make the proper decision, even when it is difficult or goes against what *"everyone"* says is the right thing to do.

Martin Luther King, the Civil Rights activist who almost single-handedly changed the course of race relations in the U.S. stated:

> *The ultimate measure of a man is not where he stands in moments of comfort, but where he stands at times of challenge and controversy.*

King was a great leader, certainly for pointing out the direction all Americans needed to follow, but more importantly, for decisively pointing it out in the face of great opposition.

The decisions we make every day may not directly influence as many people as those of Martin Luther King, but we certainly have the ability to be just as decisive by displaying the same traits of intelligence, confidence and courage so evident in King's determined decision making and leadership.

1. Think about a time you made a decision that had unintended, negative consequences. How long ago was that?_____

2. Were you able to recover from the resulting consequences in a way that left you better off than before? _____

3. Have you found that, because of past mistakes you made, you are better able to avoid future errors?_____

Successful Managers Know ...

Babe Ruth held the record for home runs hit. Even people who are not big baseball fans know that. But what is less known is that Ruth also held the record for the most strikeouts. He struck out over 1300 times. But no one who ever saw Babe Ruth swing a bat felt he had any doubt that the next swing would be a home run.

An over-emphasis on the potential negative affects (striking out) could easily have caused "analysis paralysis" on Ruth's part. Instead, he was confident in his abilities. Confidence in your decision-making can take you far. John Grisham was convinced he had written a successful book despite the fact that 45 publishers rejected his first novel, "A Time to Kill". And Dr. Suess, the famous children's writer once had 30 publisher rejections for a single story!

Even when your decisions do not immediately produce the outcome you desire, the characteristics of intelligence, courage and confidence you bring to the decision making process will ensure your long-term success, regardless of whether an individual decision immediately helps you attain your goals. Remember that your own self-confidence is what inspires other's confidence in you.

Think It Through

1. Many managers do not get immediate feedback on decisions they make. Does that ever happen to you? _____

2. Consider those who observe your decision-making. Would they prefer it if the way you make decisions was based on the length of time it takes you to receive feedback? _____.

3. Does it make sense to you that good managers would utilize the same decision-making techniques regardless of how long it takes for the full impact of their decisions to be known?

   _____

4. In addition to intelligence, courage and confidence, list three more characteristics you would want others to readily identify if they closely observed your own decision-making process.

   a. _____

   b. _____

   c. _____

Personal Challenges

- While it can be unsettling to realize that my decision-making ability is constantly on display, I will do my best to make those I lead proud of the way I make decisions.

- I know that when you help someone else up a hill, you get closer to the top yourself. I will take the time to help those I lead develop confidence in their own decision-making abilities.

Section 3

It's About Building Your Team

11

Emphasize Group Goals: Encourage the participation of all

It's Essential:

Most everyone has looked in the sky and marveled at the beauty of a flock of Canadian geese flying in their traditional "V" formation as they head south for the winter.

The "V" is no accident.

By flying in the precise pattern that is so distinctive, each bird, flapping its wings, provides lift to the bird flying behind. The result is over a 70% increase in the efficiency of flight when compared to each bird flying alone. The result: greater range with less exertion. Consequently, the distance these birds can fly is nothing short of amazing.

In business, when the activities of a group are in such sync that the actions of any one individual consistently and positively assist the efforts of others, productivity increases greatly, duplication of effort is eliminated, more gets done, and best of all, it gets done more efficiently.

If Canadian geese were like some people, the strongest of the birds might feel it was in their own best interest to go it alone. They would certainly start out quickly and would even, at first, likely leave the group far behind. Inevitably, however, as time passed, those strong but individualistic birds resting on the ground would gaze, in the same awe that overcomes each of us, at the majestic "V" formation passing over their heads.

1. Almost everyone either is currently, or has been, a member of a competitive team. Think about a time you were a team member.

2. Was it most important to you that your team would win or that you individually played a good game? _____

3. Would you enjoy being a member of a team consisting of very talented individuals if your team lost every game it played? _____

Successful Managers Know ...

Most teams are not made up of "All-Stars". Instead, teams are typically made up of individuals, each of which will likely have weaknesses as well as strengths. Inevitably, some will be more talented than others. In fact, most managers do not have the luxury of choosing every person they manage. And when they do, it is rare that each individual chosen can be a super star. Yet, unfortunately, some mangers spend precious time bemoaning the quality of their individual team members.

The best managers know, however, that it is the combined talent of the group that is important, not the talent of the group's individual members. As a result, it will be your own ability to implement the "V" that will make the difference.

The secret to implementing your own "V"?

You yourself must be completely and absolutely convinced that the individual skills of your team members are less critical to success than your own ability to develop those skills. When you demonstrate faith in your team, it can accomplish goals far beyond the highest aspirations of your team's most talented individual.

Great managers, like great coaches, do not become famous because of talented team members. Instead, they gain recognition for their own ability to convince each team member that by giving their individual best, they allow the group to soar. The pride that results is the pride that comes from team membership, not individual contribution.

Think It Through

1. Most managers will lead teams that include individuals with a variety of skill levels. Is that true of your team? _____

2. What rewards do those team members who are considered the most highly skilled regularly receive?
   _____

3. Are equal rewards regularly received by those team members who have lesser skills? _____

4. What are three additional and specific ways you could demonstrate the value of their contribution to your least skilled team members?

   a. _____

   b. _____

   c. _____

Personal Challenges

• I will make an extra effort to ensure that our team knows the goals I have set for it, and that I am committed to reaching those goals with them.

• I know I make a difference in my team members' attitudes when I show real confidence in them. I will ensure that each team member knows I value his or her contribution to the team's success.

12

Recognize Individual talents: Get the best from each team member

It's Essential:

Many people know that a carat is a measure of weight used for gemstones and is equal to 200 milligrams. When jewelers evaluate the number of carats in a diamond, weights are given to the nearest 1/100th of a carat, an amount which is called a "point." For example, a .50 carat gemstone would be called one-half carat or a 50-point stone. It might seem that the better the gem, the larger the number of carats.

While it is true that a diamond's weight (size) does impact its value, it is not the gem's only important characteristic. This is so because it is the manner in which a diamond is cut and polished that enhances its natural brilliance and shine.

Skilled jewelers know that each diamond they shape will come to them with different natural characteristics. The outcome of the jeweler's work will not be identical stones. Rather, the jeweler approaches each stone with the goal of maximizing that stone's potential and ultimate value.

In a situation similar to that faced by jewelers, your workforce will come to you consisting of individuals with many different natural characteristics. Using the same talents as the jeweler, you too must seek to reveal the maximum potential of those you lead, and as a result, enhance each individual's worth.

---

1. For some people, the biggest diamond, regardless of its quality is considered best. What do you think such individuals value most in a gem? _____

2. Some individuals seek near perfection in their gems, and thus will pay a premium for stones of the highest quality, even though the stone itself is quite small. What do you think motivates such buyers? _____?

3. Consider the group of people in your own setting. How can you best determine their value? _____

Successful Managers Know ...

The strengths needed by a group of workers are as varied as the tasks they will encounter. It's the responsibility of a good leader to recognize the complexities involved in each job (not just the required skills) and match those carefully to the natural characteristics identified in their employees.

In most organizations there is hard work to be done and the workload is multi-faceted. Your staff must be, too. A dedicated and motivated staff exists when they're confident that they can accomplish exactly what's expected of them.

As a manager seeking to maximize the effectiveness of your own work team, your job consists of four important tasks, each of which is critical to your own personal success.

• Recognize the individual strengths offered by each of your team members

- Understand that all workers have weaknesses

- Match the personal characteristics of individuals to jobs that best maximize their strengths and avoid their weaknesses

- Make sure your employees know that you feel they can succeed in their positions

An individual placed in a position where they are confident in their ability to do a good job will be highly motivated to do just that.

When you are successful in placing individuals in jobs that maximize their natural strengths, and they know they can excel, you allow your team to shine. In fact, the cluster of gems you polish will consistently display a passion that outshines any organization built around a few brilliant solitaires.

Think It Through

1. The best managers know the power of positive motivation. What factors cause you to do your best work? _____.

2. Could you excel in your job if you truly believed it was not possible for you to master it? _____.

3. What effect does your boss' belief in your abilities have on your chances of job success? _____

4. Consider your own team. What are three specific methods you can use to help them build confidence in their own abilities?

    a.   _____

    b.   _____

    c.   _____

Personal Challenges

- It has been said that "*Whether you think you can, or you think you can't, you are right*". I will do the things necessary to ensure my team always knows they can!

- It is sometimes easy to focus on an individual's flaws. I will commit to ensuring the people on my team consistently have the opportunity to demonstrate their very best features.

13

Delegate: When you can do it better yourself, don't.

It's Essential:

For most people, learning to ride a bicycle is one of those experiences they simply never forget. If you are like many, you vividly remember who it was that steadied the bike as you took your first tentative pedals. Whoever it was, it was someone you trusted with (virtually) your life!

Despite the inherent danger, the determination of children to learn to ride bikes is nothing short of amazing. It is especially so when you recognize that riding a bicycle is not one of those things people can easily be "told" how to do. Yet nearly everyone learns how.

Determined people are those who, when they reach the end of their rope, tie a knot and hang on. For most, when first learning to ride a bike, hanging on was all that could actually be done.

Once you did get the hang of bike riding, you were likely off to explore miraculous new worlds that were previously out of your reach. Perhaps the only person as proud of your accomplishment as you were, was the person who held you up during those first feeble attempts at pedaling.

When you first gained your balance, had you been able to look back at the time, you would have seen a smile rivaled only by your own. In business, delegators hold the bike; and in doing so, open new worlds for those they support.

---

1. Think about a skill you could not have acquired without a patient, but unpaid, teacher. _____

2. Why do you think, in this case, your teacher was committed to helping you? _____?

3. How do you think your teacher felt as your skill level advanced? _____

Successful Managers Know ...

Most management books, when addressing the topic of delegation, eloquently describe its many benefits. These include saving time for other important work, reducing your stress level and an increase in overall effectiveness. While these benefits of delegating are certainly real, so too are the costs of delegating.

There are real costs to delegating because, for many mangers and in many cases, the most efficient way to complete an important task is simply to do it themselves. The work will be done faster, the quality will be excellent, and you have the added advantage of absolute confidence the task has indeed been completed.

Alternatively, when you delegate, you almost always run the risk that:

The work will not be done as quickly

The quality will be less than if you did it yourself

The job may not, in fact, even get done

Consider, however, if your bicycle-riding teacher had reviewed the list above. Each of these "costs" of delegating could have been applied to bike riding. But you are probably pretty happy that your teacher paid the price. Real leaders will readily pay the cost. When they can do it better themselves, they don't, because they know that in the end both teacher and learner will be smiling.

Think It Through

1. Some managers are actually afraid to teach others because they fear it will diminish their own standing. Have you ever felt that way? _____.

2. Do you think that managers with more or less confidence in themselves are most likely to delegate? _____.

3. Consider those managers who refuse to delegate important tasks. What impact do you think that has on those they are managing? _____

4. What are three specific tasks that you currently do that could, with some instruction you could give, actually be delegated to others you lead?

    a. _____

    b. _____

    c. _____

Personal Challenges

- Refusal to delegate demonstrates a lack of confidence in myself and my training ability. I will aggressively look for areas in my job where delegation on my part could really help those I lead improve their own skills.

- I will visibly and consistently demonstrate the management philosophy of "*Each one ... teach one*" to my own work team so they too can understand the value of teaching others.

14

Train:
Give employees the knowledge and tools to do their jobs

It's Essential:

If you are like most people, you believe watching TV today is a whole lot harder than it was 40 years ago. That is not because the quality of TV shows is better or worse than before; rather, it's because simply turning on the TV set is much harder than it used to be.

In the 1960's watching TV was pretty simple. You walked over to the TV set, turned it on, and watched one of the "Big Three" networks (in the U.S., ABC, CBS, or NBC).

Contrast that to today. The number of channels offered to the average household can easily number over 100. The problem, however, is that it may also be nearly impossible to actually turn on the TV!

Today's TV includes: the TV itself, a cable box or satellite feed (for multiple channel viewing), a VCR (for old movies), a DVD (for newly released movies), *"surround sound"* (for theater quality viewing), and a CD player (for playing musical CDs).

When each of these devices is interconnected, it is easy to see why the viewer wishing simply to watch TV must choose from among four or five different remote controls, and then they must know which buttons to push. When you consider the skill and knowledge it takes to actually program and then operate all those remotes, it is easy to see why today, the existence of highly advanced tools like remote controls (without the understanding of how to properly operate them) can actually make life more, rather than less, complicated!

1. In some cases, those who seek to use a tool want to do so without first learning how it works. Consider the last electronic item you purchased. Did it come with a complete Instruction Guide or User's Manual? _____?

2. Did you thoroughly read the accompanying material before you attempted to use the item? _____

3. Do you think most people would do the same as you?
   _____

Successful Managers Know ...

The advancements in tools and technology now utilized in business have been nothing short of phenomenal. Yet, sometimes, mangers seem to yearn for "the good old days," when things were not so complicated.

The reality, however, is that once you have mastered the technology or tool, the payoff is enormous because the increases in speed, efficiency and accuracy that can be achieved by your team are nothing short of spectacular.

Consider something as non-complex as employee paychecks. In the old days, employees punched their cards, account clerks totaled employee hours, and adding machines helped calculate rates of pay. The process was time consuming, repetitive, and prone to error. Today, remarkably, employees can "punch-in" via fingerprint or even iris scanning, and computers complete the remainder of the payroll process with remarkable speed and accuracy. As a result, doing payroll today is truly much "easier" than ever before.

Management without reservations means that today, more than ever, managers simply must:

• Be on the constant lookout for advancements that can significantly improve their team's effectiveness

• Take the time they need to first learn, and then share, those advancements with their team.

It is important to recognize that implementing new tools and information will often require a significant commitment on your part. The commitment may be in time, effort, cost and sometimes, even discomfort. However, if you make that investment, and learn to master the multiple remotes of your business, you will never again want to go back to the three lonely channels featured in the good old days.

Think It Through

1. Consider your own industry. Has it significantly changed in the past 20 years? _____.

2. Name one knowledge or tool advancement that has occurred in your area of expertise that has dramatically altered the face of your own management activities. _____.

3. Some managers seem to actively avoid keeping their skills up to date. Why do you think this is so? _____.

4. What are three specific activities you can undertake to help you and your team stay up-to-date with rapid changes in the knowledge and skills they need to best do their jobs?

    a. _____

    b. _____

    c. _____

Personal Challenges

- It is important for my team and I to stay on the cutting edge of knowledge and skill in our field, and it is my job to stay sharp enough to do just that.

- Because innovation always comes from individuals, and not from bureaucracies or hierarchy, I will seek to surround myself with team members capable of creativity and innovation.

15

Communicate:
Bees do it ... so should you

It's Essential:

There is an interesting commonality between bees, ants, and industrious people. They all work together to achieve goals greater than they could individually. And they all utilize communication to do so.

Ant communication is accomplished primarily through chemicals called pheromones. When an ant finds food, she will leave a pheromone trail along the ground on her way home. In a short time, other ants follow this pheromone trail to bring back even more food.

Honeybees communicate in even more complex ways. Dr. Karl von Kirsch, an Austro-German zoologist, won the Noble Prize in 1973 for decoding the mysteries of the honeybee dance. When worker bees return to the hive with nectar and pollen, they perform one of two "dances" that communicates the direction, distance, and amount of the food available for the other bees.

The "Round dance" is used when the food source is within about 35 yards. The "Waggle dance" is used to communicate the location of food sources further away. It consists of two loops with a straight run in the middle, much like a figure eight. The direction of the straight run communicates the route to the food source while, the number of figure eights and the buzzing level employed tells the quantity of food available. It is repeated until its message is received.

Communication styles and methods may vary, from the simple to the complex, but even the most basic forms of animal life seem to understand its importance when working together.

---

1. Have you ever tried to talk to an individual who spoke only one language and that language was different from your own?

    _____

2. On a scale of 1 to 100, with 1 being very poor and 100 being very good, what number would you say best represents the quality of communication you experienced with that person? _____?

3. How much do you believe your number would have gone up if you had been able to speak the same language?

    _____

Successful Managers Know ...

To accomplish goals, you will communicate. Everyone knows that. However, communication, especially among humans, is a good deal more complex than ant scents or honeybee dances. In fact, one way to better understand human communication is to compare it to finding yourself in a large, but pitch black, room.

Any task you attempted to accomplish in such a setting would be difficult, and perhaps even dangerous. If, however, if a 15-watt light were added to the room, you would at least be aware of where you were in the room.

A 75-watt bulb would likely enable you to move about safely, but would still limit your actions.

A 150-watt bulb, however, could provide all the illumination you would need to be confident, safe, productive, efficient and effective, and thus do all that you were capable of doing.

A "Watt" is simply a measure of light and of power. The greater the wattage, the more power projected, and the more light given out. Communication is exactly like light.

When managers communicate fully, employees are illuminated and, as a result, they can better "see" and understand exactly what they need to see. The techniques managers use to add wattage to their workplace are varied, and in most cases will be more complex than the honeybee's "Waggle dance." Nevertheless, just as the bee is steadfastly committed to communication, so too are those leaders who consistently manage without reservations.

Think It Through

1. Do you think it is ever possible to "over-communicate"? _____.

2. Why do you think some managers withhold information from their team? _____.

3. If knowledge is power, what is the likely result of no communication? _____

4. What are three specific things your team absolutely must be aware of if they are to meet all of the goals you have set for them?

    a. _____

    b. _____

    c. _____

Personal Challenges

- I understand that positive messages are understood by people twice as quickly as negative ones. I will always try to keep my communication approach positive.

- Honesty in my communications characterizes my integrity. Because that is so, I will always be truthful when communicating with my work team.

Section 4

It's About Serving Your Customers

16

Be A Listener:
Listen first, talk second

It's Essential:

Communicating clearly involves important skills on the part of the individual sending the message and the individual who receives it. As a manager, it will frequently be your job to carefully listen to the messages your customers send you. Careful listening includes paying attention to what is said, how it is said, when it is said, and even the body language used by the person you are communicating with.

For managers, good customer service is no less than fulfilling customer expectations in a way that fully satisfies their needs. Because that is so, it's essential to understand that the simple action of listening is itself an important form of serving your customer.

In many cases, your customers simply want you to know how they feel. When you listen to them and show you care, you demonstrate that their feelings matter to you. By listening, you immediately elevate the stature of your customers in their own eyes, thus fulfilling their important need to feel special.

---

1. Some people consider themselves "talkers", while others consider themselves "listeners". Which label do you feel best describes you?
   _____

2. Do you know individuals who seem to talk non-stop? Do you find it easy to communicate your own ideas to such individuals? _____?

3. Consider the person you thought about in the question above. Do you find conversations with that individual enjoyable?
   _____

Successful Managers Know ...

It is important to remember that there are essentially four major factors you must consider when you decide that "listening" to your customer is a more important skill than learning to "talk" to them.

1. Recognize that it is time well spent. It may seem that you are too busy serving customers to actually listen to them, but remember that listening is one of the highest forms of customer service you can provide.

2. Recognize that listening is an active process. To be a good listener, you must show genuine interest, maintain good eye contact, avoid interrupting the speaker and ask for clarification if you do not understand the message completely. These four actions are key to active listening.

3. Smile. Be a cheerful listener. It's that simple.

4. Stay focused on the real purpose for listening. Listening is the first step in doing. Whether your customer is telling you about a complaint, making a suggestion for improvement, or giving a compliment, careful listening helps you better decide "what to do next".

Finally, recognize that listening first and talking second makes you a better manager. Doing so enables you to better understand your customers, and increased understanding means improved decision-making about how to best serve them.

Think It Through

1. Managers know that good eye contact is important for effective listening. Why do you think that is so? _____.

2. As a customer, how important is it to you to be asked open-ended questions (designed to begin a conversation) such as "How is everything?", "Can I help you find something special?", or "How may I assist you?" _____.

3. Consider those managers who primarily serve individuals within their own organization (internal customers). How important is it for managers such as these to listen first and talk second? Why?

   _____

4. Consider your own listening skills. Name three specific areas in which you believe you can improve.

   a. _____

   b. _____

   c. _____

Personal Challenges

- I will make it one of my management priorities to show respect for customers by reserving the time needed to listen carefully to what they have to say.

- Now that I fully understand the value of listening first and talking second, I will honestly reassess how others likely perceive my commitment to active listening and make improvements if necessary.

17

Show Your Customer Concern: Employees always observe your actions

It's Essential:

Despite the fact that managers often think their employees do not pay enough attention to what they say, there is no question that employees actually pay an incredible amount of attention to what their managers do. The problem, in most cases, is not that your employees will ignore you, but rather, that your employees will imitate and model your behavior very intensely.

Management must exhibit desired behaviors in an organization or employees will soon become convinced that the values expressed by their leaders are not truly embraced by them. When that is true, employees can easily get confused about how they really are supposed to treat the organization's customers.

As a manager, the message you intend to send about customer service must be the message you actually display. Every time. With every customer. When you do, you send the clear-cut signal to all who are observing that you are serious about delivering outstanding customer service. It all starts with you.

---

1. Think about a time you observed someone you worked for treating a customer very poorly. Were you surprised to see it happen? _____

2. Do you think employees in addition to yourself observed your boss's behavior in this situation? _____?

3. What message do you think your boss was sending about his or her own attitude toward providing outstanding customer service in this situation? _____

Successful Managers Know ...

As a manager, it is simply not enough to tell your employees that they must provide excellent customer service. They need to be shown "*what*" they must do to provide it and told "*why*" it is important that they do so.

Instead, some managers only teach their employees "what" they must do to enhance customer service, but neglect to tell their employees "why" it is important. These managers seem to believe that their employees will automatically understand that good guest service is important. Thus, they ignore the "why".

Actually, the "what" to do is the easy part to communicate. The "why" is much more difficult. This is so because, regardless of what is said, when they observe their managers providing poor service, they have been deprived of the "why".

Employees who have been instructed on the importance of good customer service become confused when managers demonstrate poor customer service. The employee's motivation to provide excellent service is then diminished.

Managers know that employees need to be motivated. Motivation can be expressed as:

Information about "what" to do + Understanding of "why" it is done = Motivation

The good news is the "why" can be really easy to communicate. You simply let them see you in action. If *every time* they see that excellence in customer service is important to you, it will be important to them. Every time.

The consistency you demonstrate between what you say and what you actually do is the best way to show your employees "why".

Think It Through

1. Recall a time when you were asked to complete a task, but were not told why you should do it. Would you have preferred to know exactly why you were asked to do the job?

    _____

2. If you had been told "why" it was an important task to complete, would it have affected your motivation to do a good job completing it? _____

3. Can you easily see how information about "why" a task is done results in better employee performance when completing the task?

    _____

4. Consider the customers you serve. What are three specific actions you can take to show (not tell) your employees the importance of providing outstanding customer service?

    a. _____

    b. _____

    c. _____

Personal Challenges

- I will always remember that the customer service-related actions I take represent the standard I am communicating to my employees. I always want to keep that standard very high.

- Any improvements in the customer service levels provided by my team will be the result of changes in my own actions. Enhancements of customer service levels in my own area must begin with me.

18

Customer Complaints:
Your opportunity to improve

It's Essential:

In an ongoing business, two things that are always present are your customers and the products or services you provide to them.

Good managers always want to satisfy their customers by doing their best to meet or exceed their expectations. In most cases they do. But, inevitably, sometimes customers will just not be happy with their experience with you or your company.

When that happens, you have a choice. You can react with irritation, frustration, impatience and resentment, or you can commit to utilizing their feedback to help you improve your awareness of your customers' real needs. The choice is really up to you.

When you choose to use the results of a negative customer experience to listen, learn and improve, it will help you better serve that customer. Even more importantly, if you listen carefully, you can learn things that will help you become an even better manager.

---

1. Think about the last time you were disappointed by a product or service you purchased. What one word best describes how you felt?

    _____

2. Were you hoping to find a person who would understand your problem and help you? _____

3. Do you care enough about your own customers to be that kind of person? _____

Successful Managers Know ...

That good customer relations are just as important a part of their job as making sure they deliver quality products and services.

They also know that, despite everyone's best efforts, customer complaints, legitimate or not, do occur in nearly all businesses. Because that is true, it makes the most sense for managers to view communicating with dissatisfied customers as a pro-active process that they can learn to do well.

Just as you create quality in everything else you do, you can create quality in your dealings with unhappy customers.

When you listen carefully to your customers, you can find out much about how your organization actually operates. And many of their experiences may indicate problem areas that you may not have been aware of.

When customers are dissatisfied because they were misinformed, you can use the information to improve your communication systems.

When customers are dissatisfied because they were treated poorly, you can improve your own staff training systems.

When customers are dissatisfied because they feel they did not receive value for their money, you can demonstrate your concern for their difficulty and win a customer for life by making it right for them.

Think It Through

1. Recall times when you have been approached personally by unsatisfied customers. Did most of these customers have a problem that could have been avoided if you had foreseen that it would occur?

---

2. When managers listen to customers who have difficulties, they usually can determine where the customer's problem originated. How could knowing that information help you improve your operation?

---

3. What would likely be your reaction if you saw your boss continually use customer complaints to make improvements in the area for which he or she is responsible?

---

4. What will likely be the response of your own co-workers and subordinates when they see you use customer complaints to improve your own area of responsibility?

Personal Challenges

- I will always remember that guests and customers who have a problem really need my help, and that I can learn from them.

- I will show my co-workers, by what I actually do and not just what I say, that we can improve and achieve more success when we listen to, and help, those customers who experience real problems.

19

Know Your Customer's Current Needs:
Be sensitive

It's Essential:

As managers, it sometimes becomes tempting to believe that we are in business to make a profit for our organization. Even those who work in the "public", or "non-profit" sectors of the work-world segment activities into neatly defined "profit centers". Interestingly, the famous management theorist Peter Drucker coined the term "profit center" in about 1945. Later he would write, however, "I am thoroughly ashamed of it now because, in business, there are no profit centers, only cost centers" (Drucker 2002).

What Peter Drucker came to realize, and what all managers must understand, is that their customers, not the internal workings of their business, are the source of all profits. Generally, customers are indifferent to your financial goals, costs, desired profits and challenges. They seek value for their money, and value is only created when you look outside your organization. The question to be asked is not: "What does my business seek to achieve?" but rather "What do my customers truly value?"

In the final analysis, a business does not exist to be efficient, control costs, manage people, perform accounting studies, or create fancy titles, despite all of the attention devoted to those tasks. It exists, and will continue to exist, only if it satisfies its customers needs and wants.

---

1. Think about your favorite quick service restaurant. Why is it your favorite_____?

2. Your favorite restaurant may be more or less profitable than its competitors; however, is their profitability a concern to you when you choose to go there? _____?

3. Based on your answers to these questions, if you managed your favorite quick service restaurant, should you be more sensitive to your customer's needs or your own profit margins?

_____

Successful Managers Know ...

It is one thing for a manager to recognize the importance of satisfying customer needs; it is sometimes quite another to assess the satisfaction levels you and your work team actually achieve.

As you have learned in this book, sometimes the most effective way to assess your success in meeting your customers' needs is to "listen first" when you talk to them. Speaking to customers is always a good idea; however, many managers have found it helpful to use additional tools when measuring guest satisfaction.

Former New York City Mayor Ed Koch is famous for his question "How'm I doin?" when asking the citizens of New York to assess his performance. He was on the right track because asking the question "How are we doing?" is an important part of the continuous quality improvement process.

Guest comment cards, mystery shoppers, report cards, surveys, and suggestion boxes are all credible measurement tools used by managers to stay abreast of their guests' needs, wants, and desires. As an effective manager, an important part of your job is maintaining a system of customer feedback that allows you to truly "know" those you serve.

Think It Through

1. Consider the main measurement you use to assess your own success in meeting your customers' needs. Is movement in that measurement shared with those you manage? _____ Should it be? _____

2. How do you feel when your own boss gives you a specific and measurable goal to achieve and you successfully achieve it? _____.

3. Why do you think, in the majority of cases, managers who give their employees specific and achievable goals enjoy higher productivity levels than those managers who do not? _____.

4. Re-consider your answer to the first of these questions. Name three additional measures you could you to assess how well you are doing at meeting the needs of you customers.

   a. _____

   b. _____

   c. _____

Personal Challenges

- I will make it a priority to review (and improve if needed), the procedures I have established for measuring customer satisfaction levels achieved by my team.

- I will share with my team, on a regular basis, the progress we are making toward meeting our own guest satisfaction goals.

20

Anticipate Your Customer's Future Needs: Be Perceptive

It's Essential:

For many years, the single most popular item on American restaurant menus has been the hamburger. Consider "Joe's Diner," a popular restaurant operated in 1955. The restaurant was very successful and its best selling item was a hand-made hamburger. Because it was so popular, the manager and staff spent a great deal of time perfecting its production. In fact, after years of hard work, the hamburger served at Joe's Diner was tasty, served piping hot, sold at a fair price and generated an excellent profit.

That restaurant's managers and staff may have been working so hard on perfecting what they were already doing, they might have been forgiven for not noticing that Ray Kroc opened the first McDonalds restaurant in Des Plaines, Illinois on April 15th. 1955.

McDonald's restaurants are now operated in over 115 countries worldwide and serve more than 50 million customers per day. McDonalds operates or franchises more than 13,500 restaurants in the United States but an even larger number of stores now exist *outside* the U.S.

Despite the continued popularity of McDonalds, the hamburger they produced then, and now, is probably not of the same superior quality as that served at Joe's Diner. But McDonalds probably took a great number of Joe's customers.

Why?

Because Joe's Diner was focusing on the internal workings of its business, rather than the emerging and changing needs of its customers. Doing so is nearly always fatal in any industry where change is rapid and continual.

---

1. Most observers would agree that people today are likely no more, or less, thirsty than they were 50 years ago. But think about the serving sizes of current day soft drinks. Do you believe these serving sizes are larger today than they were 50 years ago. _____?

2. What factors likely caused today's consumers to desire such large beverage sizes? _____?

3. How successful do you believe a soft drink vendor would be today, if they still served their product in the same container size as they did in the 1950's? _____?

Successful Managers Know ...

The product or service provided to a customer is only as good as its ability to meet that customer's needs. Managing without reservations requires that you understand this is true regardless of a product's quality level. As the auto industry developed in the U.S., even the best-made buggy whip was simply of no value to the driver of a car.

The key to anticipating your customer's future needs is to focus on the value your customers place on your product or service, not the product or service itself.

To stay ahead of the customer change curve, stay focused on the answers to these questions:

- *"Why do my customers value what I do?"*

- *"Will those customers value the same things in the future?"*

- *"What specific activities do I regularly undertake to track changes occurring in the wants and needs of my customer?"*

- *"How can I ensure that the product or service I provide changes in accordance with my customers' needs?"*

A valuable principle for all managers to remember is that the only thing that will not change is the fact that everything continues to change.

Think It Through

1. Do you agree that change, in most cases, improves the products and services customers buy? _____

2. If change brings improvement, who do you think should be responsible for identifying and initiating needed change?

   a. _____

   b. _____

   c. _____

3. Do you think your customers count on you to look out for their changing needs? _____

4. Do you think your business counts on you to set, as a major priority, seeking to identify the changing needs of your customers?

   _____

Personal Challenges

- I will remember that an obsessive compulsion toward doing things right can sometimes reduce my effectiveness in doing the right things.

- I will strive to keep my team focused on our customers' future, as well as their current need for what we produce.

Section 5

It's About Knowing Your Goals

21

Recognize Company Goals: Understand how they define success

It's Essential:

In 1903, the Wright brothers' first successful flight in Kitty Hawk, North Carolina marked the beginning of the aviation industry. Interestingly, one of the biggest factors in the growth of the air transportation was the U.S. Postal Service. The Kelly Airmail Act of 1925 provided private airlines the opportunity to function as mail carriers. These private carriers, using their "air-mail" revenue, eventually added passenger service.

Today, airlines in the US carry more than 650 million passengers per year. Their goal is to do so safely. To that end, travelers are subjected to specific, and strictly enforced, rules and regulations. For example, it's essential that travelers have a valid ticket and boarding pass, provide a form of photo identification, arrive one hour before a flight (two hours for international flights), stay within clearly defined luggage size and weight restrictions, and ensure that carry on items comply with stringent Federal requirements.

Air travel is popular because it is fast and convenient. To take advantage of those benefits, however, you must follow the rules that govern air travel. Regardless of your own ideas about how flights should be operated, if you follow the rules, you get on the plane; if you do not, you will be denied boarding.

Life is like that.

In many cases, someone other than you will determine what you may and may not do. When you understand what others demand of you, you can choose to follow the rules and get where you want to go.

---

1. Remember the time when you first learned to drive. Were you nervous? _____

2. Recall when you began to learn to follow traffic rules and regulations. How critical was knowledge of these rules to getting where you wanted to go safely? _____?

3. If you were teaching someone to drive, how important would it be for you to teach them traffic rules and regulations, in addition to steering and stopping the car? _____

Successful Managers Know ...

Some managers find themselves in regular confrontations with their bosses. These situations are usually non-productive and simply result in wasted emotional energy.

As a member of a team, it is your responsibility to fully understand exactly how your organization defines a successful leader. If you are like most managers, you will find that within your organization there are "negotiables" and "non-negotiables".

The negotiables help define the areas in which leaders are allowed freedom to operate, and most leaders, of course, revel in these. The non-negotiables, however, are even more important to understand. They are the success strategies that are so important to the organization that they simply must be followed. Every time.

Those who follow the rules, gain the organization's rewards. Those, however, who do not take the time to discover how their organization defines success, will rarely achieve it.

Think It Through

1. While most managers appreciate loyalty in their employees, how would you feel about an employee who continually questioned and criticized the goals you have established for your team? _____.

2. Do you feel most mangers expect to achieve "blind" devotion in their employees? _____.

3. Do you believe that good managers allow their employees to ask legitimate questions about the direction in which these managers are leading their teams? _____

4. Name three specific ways you could seek clarification from your own boss about the goals that have been set for you or your team

   a. _____

   b. _____

   c. _____

Personal Challenges

- I understand that the leaders of my organization have definitions for success I simply must understand. If I do not, I will respectfully seek clarification about them.

- I understand that, as a leader of my organization, my team members must understand my definitions of success. If they do not, it is my job to provide ways for them to respectfully seek clarification.

22

Recognize Your Goals: Understand how you define success

It's Essential:

There are few things in life that are as exciting as planning a vacation. When preparing for the trip, there is always happiness, excitement and the anticipation of future delight.

If your trip includes air travel, you can choose to depart from, or arrive at, over 19,000 airports in the U.S. alone. Your destination choices are nothing less than extraordinary. While the restrictions at each airport you use will be the same, the vacation destination you select is entirely up to you because only you can decide where you want to go, and how you want to get there.

Once you decide what will make a successful vacation for you, whether your choice is the beach, the mountains, a large city, or the country, you are then free to make and follow a plan that will take you there.

In many ways, life is like arranging a vacation. There are countless destinations, as well as great things to see and do along the way. Fortunately, for all of us, our entire lives are our exclusive vacation; we choose our own destinations, make our own plans, and then set out to discover the world on our own unique journey.

1. Consider the most successful person you know. Do you seek the same type of success? _____

2. Assume you achieved the same measure of success. Are there any aspects of that person's life you would change, and thus improve, if you could? _____

3. Do you believe that the definition of success you hold would apply to every other person you know? _____

Successful Managers Know ...

In business, your company's definition of success may be measured in finite terms such as increases in sales achieved, profits generated or production quotas met. While these are important, none of them, alone, is likely to provide you the motivation or passion you need to become the very best of the "best" managers. Achieving these goals may constitute the company's non-negotiable definition of success, but unless you personalize them, they will not provide the drive you need to excel.

In fact, it is the goals you set for yourself, not those that are set for you by others that will most drive you to succeed. The best managers consistently individualize their work environment. They instinctively know that their own pride and passion are the secrets to success.

You must realize that you have a personal need for accomplishment and recognition in addition to what your company expects from you. By finding what truly motivates you and using that passion to energize your activities, you will not be driven by your company's expectations, but will experience the joy at work that will drive you to more success than you ever expected.

Think It Through

1. Do you feel that your own bosses understand the factors you use to define personal success? _____.

2. Who is primarily responsible for ensuring the definitions of success used by your organization match those of your own? _____.

3. Is it reasonable to believe that all the success you seek in life must come from your employment? _____

4. In addition to your pay, what are the top three things you need to receive from your job if you are to feel it contributes to your personal success?

    a. _____

    b. _____

    c. _____

Personal Challenges

- I will remember that success is determined by two things. How far I go and how far I have traveled from where I started.

- My team members have their own aspirations for success. I will make it a priority to assist them in achieving their definitions of success, as well as those of our organization.

23

Expect Success: Positive thinking and positive doing

It's Essential:

The expectation of positive results leads to positive results. To better understand this universal truth, consider the way parents teach their toddlers how to walk. When the child is just taking his or her first steps, the positive parent reaction is an enthusiastic:

- "You can do it!
- "You're doing great!"
- "Look how well you are doing"
- "I'm so proud of you, you took your first step"

Moreover, all the while the parents are there to catch the toddlers when they, inevitably, fall. These parents are not merely optimistic. Despite the fact that their child has never before walked, they are certain that ultimately their children will indeed learn how.

You would never hear a caring parent say:

- "You can't walk, why are you even trying?

- "You're still falling down. You should stop trying right now!"

- "You're no good at walking, you'll never learn!"

- "I'm too busy to show you how to walk; I've got my own job to do!"

In your life, and in the lives of those around you, a positive reaction to life leads to the positive actions that ultimately result in success. Negative attitudes make it easy to quit and, as a result, fail at those same tasks the positive person ultimately accomplishes.

---

1. Have you ever worked hard to learn a skill that took a lot of effort before you mastered it? _____

2. Do you ever consider giving up on learning that skill? _____

3. What precisely, do you think, caused you to continue until you were successful at mastering the skill? _____

Successful Managers Know ...

Every situation in life can be viewed in a positive light. When you unwaveringly focus on the positive aspects of the situations you face, you are not ignoring the negative aspects; you are simply choosing to recognize that it is your attitude, not your circumstances, that define your reality.

In the classic 1946 Frank Capra movie, "It's A Wonderful Life", Jimmy Stewart's character George Bailey re-discovers the value and beauty of life. He does so despite his character's disappointments and trials, but only when his guardian angel is able to re-direct his attention from the negatives of his life to all of its positives; positives that George Bailey readily overlooked.

When Christopher Reeves (the actor famous for playing Superman in the movies) was, in real-life, completely paralyzed from the neck down in a horse riding accident at the age of 43, it was, no doubt, incredibly tragic.

Those who followed Reeves' heroic efforts after the accident, however, know that he did not permit himself to become the victim of this tragedy. He found his situation to be one in which his own courage, coupled with an extraordinarily positive view of life, allowed him to provide hope and inspiration to the lives of millions of people with a strength that Superman could only envy.

Do you find difficulty in your life as a manager? Likely you will.

Despite that, you can focus on the positives of your situation. And you can do it regardless of the circumstances you face. When you do, you will summon the inner strength you need to add positive doing to your positive thinking and, as a result, conquer any circumstances you face.

Think It Through

1. One characteristic of effective leaders is their ability to respond positively even in trying situations. Do you believe you are that type of leader? _____ .

2. Consider a time when you needed to show leadership in a difficult situation. What personal characteristic do you think most allowed you to do so? _____ .

3. Would you agree with the statement that: *"Leaders display their best, or their worst, qualities when leading through tough times"*. _____ ?
   Why or why not? _____

4. Assume for a moment that, due to no fault of your own, you lost your current job. What could be three very positive aspects of such a set of circumstances?

   a. _____

   b. _____

   c. _____

Personal Challenges

- Courage has been defined, "*not as lack of fear, but rather, as positive action in the face of fear.*" I will remain courageous regardless of my circumstances.

- My team counts on me to remain positive, especially when circumstances are difficult. I will remember that, as a leader, my performance and attitude will directly affect theirs.

24

Think Creatively: Explore outside the box

It's Essential:

Ivan Pavlov the Nobel prize winning Russian and B.F. Skinner, the Harvard Professor from Susquehanna, Pennsylvania are both known for their work studying the phenomenon known as "conditioning". Pavlov used dogs in his studies, while Skinner used pigeons. Most people know the studies concluded that a behavior, when positively reinforced (rewarded), tended to be repeated; while a behavior that was not rewarded, or that was punished, tended not to be repeated.

What is lesser know about conditioning is the result which occurs when random behavior is rewarded. For example, Skinner found that, in a group of pigeons, when food was randomly dispensed, the pigeons began behaving as if there were a relationship between the presentation of the food and what they were doing at the exact time the food as dispensed. The result; various pigeons, each performing different activities, but each convinced their own activity would result in a reward.

Like the pigeons, people often observe their own world and truly believe there is a relationship between what they are doing and the results they seek. In most cases, however, it takes a courageous person to reject the "old ways" in favor of the "new," especially when the results that will be achieved are unknown. The most successful people, however, not only look at the tried and true way of doing things; they also look for the new truth to try.

1. Many times, gamblers believe they own a lucky hat, pair of socks, shirt or other item. Do you understand why such people believe wearing their "lucky" item will make their gambling odds better?

_____

2. The pigeons in the Skinner experiment also believed that what they were doing at the time they were randomly rewarded with a food pellet caused them to have good luck. Do you see the similarities in these two situations? _____

3. While there is certainly no direct physical harm in believing that a hat or any other article of clothing is "lucky," do you think that those who believe in such things sometimes act on their beliefs in ways that, in fact, result in negative outcomes? _____.

Successful Managers Know ...

In many cases, mangers deal with routine problems. Often however, the challenges managers face in achieving their goals are new to them and to the team they lead.

In those situations, some mangers believe the biggest obstacle they face is that of knowing exactly what to do. The best managers, however, realize that the greatest challenge they face in such a situation is fear of failure.

Failure, in the short run, is something all managers encounter and, ultimately, overcome. This so because, in management, as in life, failure is not something they can eliminate; it is something they rise above. In fact, instead of defining failure as a blunder, the best managers positively define failure as *"the wonderful discovery of what did not work!"*

Insisting that, when their efforts do not meet with immediate success, they will only generate new ideas and employ new efforts, these managers think outside the box continually.

The end result they achieve is not failure, but the wisdom that comes from experiencing life's challenges and confidently trusting that their efforts will, ultimately, lead to the achievement of their highest goals.

Think It Through

1. Scientists often use trial and error in their experiments because they know that each alternative they eliminate (each failure) brings them one step closer to success. Do you understand why they would feel that way? _____.

2. Successful salespersons are fond of saying they do not mind a "No" response from potential buyers because, statistically, each "No" brings them one customer closer to a "Yes", and thus a sale. Do you understand why they would feel that way? _____.

3. Do you think that the philosophy *"failure is simply one stop on the road to success"* can be applied to your own job?

   _____

4. Consider your current career choice. List two specific times in which your initial effort at addressing a problem did not work as well as your later efforts (i.e. where you learned from your past mistakes).

   a. _____

   b. _____

Personal Challenges

- I will recall that a manager who has never made mistakes is likely a manager who lacked the creativity to try new things. I will seek to be a creative manager.

- One of the greatest mistakes I can make is that of robbing my team of their own creativity. I will make sure each of my team members knows that honest mistakes made in the passionate pursuit of our goals are a positive thing.

25

Treasure the Awe:
Life is a mystery to be lived

It's Essential:

Those who live complete lives understand that life is an adventure so vast that it never ends.

Interestingly, in most cases, when people are asked to look back on their lives, the things they identify as being the most incredible parts of their journey, and those that made the biggest impact on them, are not necessarily those things that seemed most significant when they were younger.

Those who have lived full lives consistently mention those unique life experiences that brought them joy or unexpected delight. These include experiences that, in hindsight, were quite remarkable; such as:

• The majesty of nature

- The innocence of a child

- The unexpected generosity of a stranger

- The loyalty of a good friend

- The inspiration that results from heroism

- The simplicity of goodness

To live richly, its essential to recognize that life is full of many good things, and as Mae West, the popular 1930's actress, was famously quoted, "Too much of a good thing, is simply wonderful".

1. What are the things you appreciate most about your own life? _____

2. Are there specific individuals who contribute to the things you identified? _____?

3. Do you take the time, regularly, to tell those people how much they really mean to you? _____

Successful Managers Know ...

Managers often see themselves as problem solvers. Those who manage without reservations, however, understand that life is a mystery to be lived, not a problem to be solved. This is so because management is simply a microcosm of life.

Yes, problems must be addressed and goals must be achieved, but not to the extent that the journey itself is unappreciated. Too often, managers focus on material accomplishments, rather than recall the conversation between two men as they watched the passing of the wealthiest man in town's funeral procession.

"How much did he leave?" asked the first man.

"He left it all." replied the second.

Successful managers do not allow themselves to become so busy reaching material goals that they stop recognizing the magnificence of life. And that magnificence will be on display at work as well as at home.

The kindness shown to a co-worker, the sharing of joy and sorrows with friends at work, the sheer pride that comes with a job well-done, or even the calmness of a cup of coffee at the end of a busy day are all important accomplishments that can be recognized, cherished and daily celebrated on your life's journey. Enjoy your trip.

Think It Through

1. Successful managers know their most valuable possessions are experiences, not things. Is that true for you?

    _____.

2. How do the goals managers set for themselves influence their priorities in life and work?

    _____.

3. What are two specific past events that have made the most positive impact on your own life?

    a. _____

    b. _____

4. What are two specific future events you believe would most define success in your own life?

    a. _____

    b. _____

Personal Challenges

- I will make it one of my management priorities to realize that it is the people I affect, and how I affect them, that will comprise my own leadership legacy.

- In my own life's journey, I resolve to relish the splendor of the trip, and not focus on the troubles I may encounter along the way.

978-0-595-44053-5
0-595-44053-3

www.ingramcontent.com/pod-product-compliance
Lightning Source LLC
Chambersburg PA
CBHW030851180526
45163CB00004B/1530

* 9 7 8 0 5 9 5 4 4 0 5 3 5 *